ANIMALS
on the Trail with
LEWIS AND CLARK

DOROTHY HINSHAW PATENT

Photographs by WILLIAM MUÑOZ

CLARION BOOKS • NEW YORK

Clarion Books
a Houghton Mifflin Company imprint
215 Park Avenue South, New York, NY 10003
Text copyright © 2002 by Dorothy Hinshaw Patent
Photographs copyright © 2002 by William Muñoz

Additional photograph credits:
American Philosophical Society Library: pages 91, 103
Charles, Darwin, *Journal of Researches*: page 8
Library of Congress: page xii
Montana Historical Society: page 66
National Exposures, Daniel J. Cox: pages 5, 75
National Museum of American Art, Washington DC/Art Resource, NY: page 30
Collection of the New-York Historical Society, 1971.125: page 63
Stark Museum of Art: page 77

The text was set in 15-point Breughel.
Maps on pages viii-ix and 97 by Kayley LeFavier

For information about permission to reproduce selections from this book, write to Permissions,
Houghton Mifflin Company, 215 Park Avenue South, New York, NY 10003.

www.houghtonmifflinbooks.com

Printed in Singapore

Library of Congress Cataloging-in-Publication Data
Patent, Dorothy Hinshaw.
Animals on the trail with Lewis and Clark / Dorothy Hinshaw Patent ;
photos by William Munoz.
p.   cm.
Includes bibliographical references (p.   ) and index.
Summary: Retraces the Lewis and Clark journey and blends their observations of
previously unknown animals with modern information about those same animals.
ISBN 0-395-91415-9
1. Lewis and Clark Expedition (1804–1806)—Juvenile literature. 2. Animals—West
(U.S.)—History—19th century—Juvenile literature. 3. West (U.S.)—Description and
travel—Juvenile literature. 4. Natural history—West (U.S.)—History—19th century—Juvenile
literature. 5. Natural history—West (U.S.)—History—19th century. [1. Lewis and Clark
Expedition (1804–1806) 2. Animals—West (U.S.)—History—19th century 3. West
(U.S.)—Description and travel.] I. Munoz, William, ill. II. Title.
F592.7 .P37 2002
917.804'2—dc21
2001042200

TWP 10 9 8 7 6 5 4 3 2 1

To all those who help educate people about
the amazing journey of Lewis and Clark

Contents

Acknowledgments

The author wishes to thank Chuck Sundstrom for reading the manuscript and making suggestions and for providing the list of animals described in the journals.

Thanks also to George Knapp and the Travelers' Rest Chapter of the Lewis and Clark Trail Heritage Foundation for the opportunity to photograph replicas of expedition equipment.

Author's Note

It's important to keep in mind while reading this book that Native American people lived in close contact with the natural world and knew all the animals encountered by the Corps of Discovery very, very well. The few people of European descent who had seen some of these animals were not concerned with describing them for science. Grizzlies and pronghorn, for example, had been noticed by the Spanish, and fur traders were familiar with the prairie dog. But no one before Lewis had set out to catalog and describe the animals of the American West. Only rarely did Lewis provide a name for the species he found. More often, he used a descriptive term for them, such as "small brown pheasant" for what we now call Richardson's blue grouse, and "prairie hen with pointed tail" for the sharp-tailed grouse.

In the text, I have quoted occasionally from the journals of Lewis and Clark. I have corrected the spelling and grammar where necessary to make the excerpts easier to read.

The name of the Shoshone woman who accompanied the Corps of Discovery has been spelled more than a dozen different ways. Most white scholars of Lewis and Clark today spell the name "Sacagawea," as it is spelled in this book. This spelling is based on the Mandan version of her name, which means "Bird Woman." The Lemhi Shoshone Indians, who are the descendants of her tribe, prefer to spell her name "Sacajawea," which means "One Who Carries a Burden" in their language.

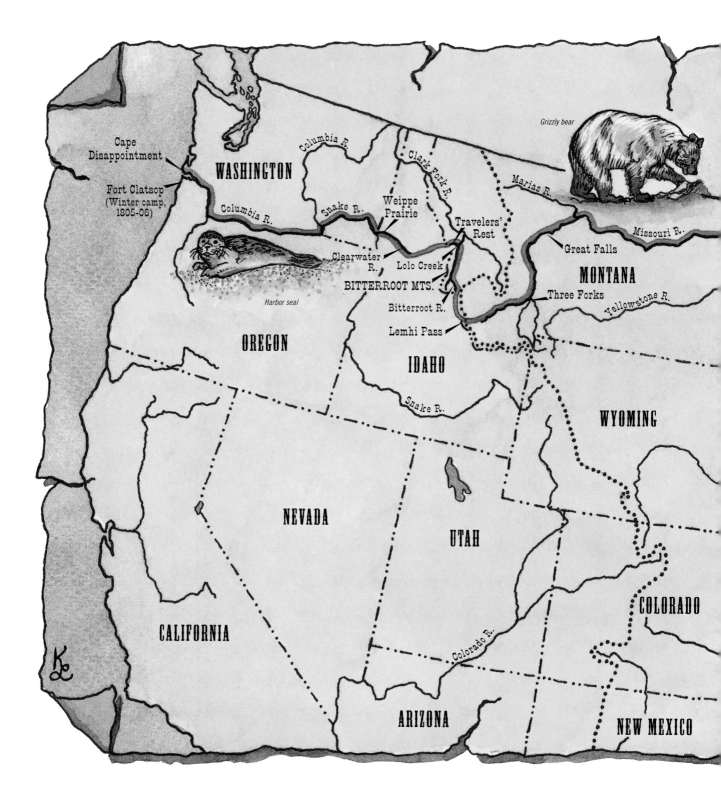

Cape
Disappointment

Fort Clatsop
(Winter camp,
1805-06)

WASHINGTON

Grizzly bear

Columbia R.

Clark Fork R.

Marias R.

Columbia R.

Snake R.

Weippe
Prairie

Travelers'
Rest

Missouri R.

Great Falls

Clearwater
R.

Lolo Creek

BITTERROOT MTS.

MONTANA

Three Forks

Yellowstone R.

Harbor seal

Bitterroot R.

OREGON

Lemhi Pass

IDAHO

Snake R.

WYOMING

NEVADA

UTAH

CALIFORNIA

COLORADO

Colorado R.

ARIZONA

NEW MEXICO

CANADA

Buffalo

Fort Mandan
(Winter camp,
1804-05)

NORTH
DAKOTA

SOUTH
DAKOTA

*Black-tailed
prairie dog*

MINNESOTA

WISCONSIN

Mississippi R.

MICHIGAN

NEBRASKA

Hill of the
Little Devils

Missouri R.

IOWA

Platte R.

ILLINOIS

INDIANA

KANSAS

*Great Plains
wolf*

Arkansas R.

Camp
Dubois

Ohio R.

St. Louis

MISSOURI

KENTUCKY

OKLAHOMA

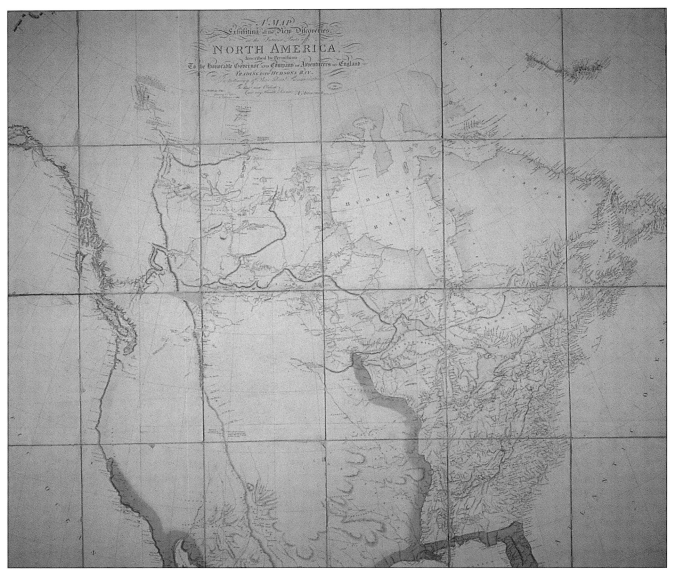

The western two-thirds of North America was a blank area on maps before Lewis and Clark's expedition.

1

Journey of Discovery

Thomas Jefferson, who became president of the United States in 1801, possessed unbounded curiosity about the vast unknown region that stretched from the Mississippi River to the Rocky Mountains and on to the Pacific Ocean. At the time, the United States consisted of only sixteen states and ended on the eastern banks of the Mississippi. On the other side, by the mouth of the Missouri River, the bustling frontier town of St. Louis hosted French fur trappers who braved the wilds to harvest beaver and other animals. These trappers were the only white men who knew much about the territory along the Missouri River.

In 1802, Jefferson decided to send a man named Meriwether Lewis westward to explore the unknown territory. Lewis, a former army captain who had left active military duty to serve as Jefferson's private secretary, was to lead an expedition across the continent to explore the Missouri River, cross the Rockies, and descend along the Columbia River to the Pacific Ocean. Traders, fur trappers, and explorers had traveled as far as the mouth of the Columbia, so Jefferson knew that the distance from St. Louis to the Pacific Ocean was approximately two thousand miles. That was about all he knew of the American West, except that the land was inhabited by Indians.

The Missouri River, shown here near Omaha, Nebraska, crosses six states before it empties into the Mississippi River.

Before Lewis and Clark crossed the continent, European Americans
had never seen tall, craggy mountains like the Rockies.

Jefferson felt confident that the future of the United States lay to the west. Foremost in his mind was the hope that the explorers would find a water route connecting the Missouri River with the Columbia. In those days almost all trade goods traveled by water. Few roads existed, and there were no railroads. Boats provided the only practical way to transport heavy cargo over long distances. If they could navigate most of the way through the Rocky Mountains, trade between the

The Columbia River flows between the present states of Oregon and Washington before emptying into the Pacific Ocean.

eastern and western parts of North America and across the Pacific to Asia would then be practical. Jefferson hoped Lewis would find such a route.

Jefferson wanted to establish peaceful relations with the Indians and trade with them. The more he knew about them and their relationship to their environment, the better. How did the Indians hunt and fish? What goods did they trade among themselves?

Everything about the West drew Jefferson's curiosity. The wildlife of the region especially fascinated him. He knew that this unknown land must possess a wealth of animal life, including vast numbers of fur-bearing animals that could enhance the economy of the young country.

Jefferson's curiosity was scientific as well as practical. He knew about the buffalo that lived in the West. They had once thrived east of the Mississippi but had been pushed out by human settlement. What animals shared the landscape with

Beaver pelts were a major reason for the interest in the West.

European Americans knew of buffalo before the Lewis and Clark expedition; these powerful animals had lived east of the Mississippi before whites settled there.

beaver and buffalo? Were there wolves and deer? Geese and swans? And were there animals yet unknown to science? Lewis was instructed to collect specimens of the animals he found and to describe them.

Jefferson had helped dig up the bones of a huge animal named *Megalonyx* in what is now West Virginia. The creature was unlike any known animal, and Jefferson hoped that Lewis might find living specimens on his trek. Maybe Lewis would also find living mastodons, ancient members of the elephant family that once lived across North America. The concept of extinction was very new to science in the early 1800s, so it wasn't strange for Jefferson to believe that such animals might still roam the vast unexplored expanse of the West. Today we know that *Megalonyx* was an extinct giant ground sloth and that mastodons had died out thousands of years before.

Jefferson taught Lewis a great deal about science. He also sent him to Philadelphia in March of 1803 to meet with some of the country's leading scientists. There, at the American Philosophical Society, the most distinguished scientists of the time presented their findings. Benjamin Smith Barton, professor of botany at the University of Pennsylvania, showed Lewis how to preserve plant and animal specimens and how to label them correctly. Dr. Caspar Wistar, physician and expert on fossils, discussed mastodons and *Megalonyx* with Lewis, telling him what was known about these animals from their bones. And Dr. Benjamin Rush provided him with medicines for the journey and gave him a list of questions to ask the Indians.

While Lewis prepared for his expedition, Jefferson was busy arranging one of the most important political deals ever made.

Ground sloths lived in America thousands of years ago; Jefferson hoped the Corps of Discovery might find them alive in the West.

Spain, which had once owned the Louisiana Territory, had secretly turned it over to France. Jefferson did not trust the French leader, Napoleon, and he offered to buy the port of New Orleans, which was vital to American trade. Napoleon responded by offering the entire territory, which stretched all the way north from the Gulf Coast to the British lands near what is now the Canadian border, and all the way west from the Mississippi River to what we now call the Continental Divide. The Continental Divide is the line dividing waters that flow into the Pacific Ocean from those that flow eastward. Jefferson jumped at the opportunity. The United States paid only $15 million for this land. The deal, which was completed on April 30, 1803, became known as the Louisiana Purchase. It instantly doubled the size of the country.

Lewis and his expedition would therefore be exploring American territory, not foreign lands, during the first part of their journey. With the Louisiana Purchase, Jefferson became even more eager for Lewis to get on his way to find out what lay to the west.

Lewis hoped to begin his journey early in the summer of 1803, but all the detailed preparations took longer than expected. Men had to be recruited and supplies gathered. The expedition would be completely out of touch for many months, so Lewis needed to buy everything from fish hooks to candles to needles and thread. Guns, ammunition, scientific instruments, clothing, gifts for the Indians, medicines, and all sorts of other items needed to be purchased. While Lewis assumed that hunting would supply a significant amount of the necessary food, he also had to bring along rations for times when no game could be found. Cornmeal, lard, flour, salt pork, and smaller amounts of other foods had to be procured. The amount of goods brought along on the expedition was enormous, including seven tons of food alone!

Jefferson and Lewis decided that someone was needed to share the command of the expedition. What if Lewis were wounded, became seriously ill, or even died? They turned to William Clark, who had once been Lewis's commanding officer in the army. Clark had had wilderness experience on the Kentucky frontier and in military campaigns against Indians in the Ohio Valley. He was an excellent mapmaker and a better surveyor than Lewis. The two men complemented each other in their abilities, and each trusted the other completely.

The men divided up their duties. Lewis was to focus his observations on natural history, Clark was assigned the job of making maps, and both men were to keep journals describing what they experienced. Several of the other men kept journals as well. While some of the men who would accompany them had already been chosen, the leaders realized they would need still more help to accomplish their mission.

In November 1803, the group, known as the Corps of Dis-

The men wrote in their journals using quill pens. Lewis and Clark each started out with a lap desk, which made the writing easier. At night, they had to write by candlelight.

covery, camped for the winter by the Wood River in Illinois, on the eastern shore of the Mississippi River near St. Louis. Their temporary home is now called Camp Wood or Camp Dubois. The adventurers kept busy with preparations, and Lewis visited St. Louis frequently to recruit more men and to purchase additional supplies. Finally, on May 14, 1804, the expedition departed from Camp Dubois. Their great adventure had begun.

#

Through Plains and Prairies

After leaving their winter camp, the Corps of Discovery crossed the Mississippi River and headed west up the Missouri River. About forty men—no one knows exactly how many—accompanied by Lewis's Newfoundland dog, Seaman, traveled in three boats: a large wooden keelboat and two flat-bottomed rowboats called pirogues. They had to fight the current and watch out for dead trees and sandbars in the water. During this first leg of the journey, they averaged only about ten difficult miles a day in what was now stifling heat. When the wind was strong enough, they could hoist sail to help propel the boats up

Tallgrass prairie stretches across the eastern side of the Great Plains.

the river. But most of the time the men had to paddle and pole with all their might to make any progress.

They left the settled area around St. Louis near the mouth of the Missouri, and the woods gradually dwindled and gave way to the tallgrass prairie. Tallgrasses made up the easternmost part of the gigantic expanse of land that formed the heartland of North America before European settlement. From Saskatchewan and Alberta in Canada almost to the Mexican border, and from Indiana to the Rockies, grass stretched in all directions, relieved only by the ribbons of trees lining the banks of rivers and streams.

The tallgrass prairie covered a section of Ohio, almost all of Indiana, Illinois, and Iowa, half of Missouri, and part of Minnesota. The tallgrasses stood six to eight feet high. This rich area could be turned into desirable farmland. Towns and farms had already begun to dot the tallgrass landscape east of the Mississippi. Indeed, Ohio had been added as the seventeenth state in 1803.

As the explorers struggled up the Missouri River, they encountered an abundance of creatures already familiar to science. One day, they came across a three-mile-long blanket of white feathers covering the river. Soon the men found the source: a sandbar, where countless white pelicans rested to shed their old feathers and grow new ones. Lewis wanted a specimen. Even though the clouds of pestering mosquitoes were so thick that he couldn't aim his gun well, he fired blindly into the dense flock and killed one of the pelicans—they were packed together so tightly he could hardly miss. He poured water into the expandable beak pouch and found that it could hold five gallons.

Soon the Corps of Discovery reached the western edge of

White pelicans often gather together in large groups. This photo was taken at a pelican rookery (breeding site) in Montana.

the tallgrass and entered the Great Plains, the heart of the American prairie. At about the ninety-eighth meridian of longitude, the average annual rainfall becomes so reduced that tallgrass can no longer dominate the landscape. As little as fourteen inches of rain per year falls on parts of this land. The wind blows more strongly as well, carrying away much of the moisture. This mixed-grass region, which stretches west through the middle tier of states from North Dakota into

The mixed-grass prairie is home to especially abundant plant and animal life.

Texas, was home to many plants and animals not known in the United States at that time.

The tree-lined riverbanks blocked the men's view of the prairie as they traveled along the river, although sometimes the lay of the land allowed them to see beyond the water, including the sight of large herds of buffalo. But they had no overview. Their first chance came when they reached a tall mound near the river and could climb up and take in the landscape. The Indians feared the spot, believing that tiny humanlike devils with sharp arrows lived there. Clark called it the Hill of the Little Devils on the map he made. The town of Vermillion, South Dakota, now lies nearby, and the hill bears the name Spirit Mound.

Lewis, Clark, and eleven of the men climbed the mound on August 25, 1804. Standing on the summit they could see for the first time the expanse of prairie below. "From the top of this mound we beheld a most beautiful landscape; numerous herds of buffalo were seen feeding in various directions. The plain to north, northwest, and northeast extends without interruption as far as can be seen," wrote Clark. He counted buffalo and elk "upwards of 800 in number." He also com-

When the men were able to climb up on bluffs and hills, they could see buffalo grazing nearby.

mented that the only trees to be seen clung to the banks of the river and the creeks.

Bird life abounded on the Hill of the Little Devils. The prairie wind blew many insects into the face of the mound, and large numbers of swallows dipped and dived, scooping up the insects in flight. Blackbirds, meadowlarks, and wrens also inhabited the hill.

As the expedition continued up the river, the men were amazed at the natural bounty of fruit and game. European Americans had seen nothing like the abundance of prairie life. The explorers commented on it over and over in their journals.

New finds came thick and fast during September 1804. On September 7, while Lewis and Clark were walking through the grassland, they found themselves in a landscape of earthen mounds and burrows. Small animals that looked like ground squirrels sat on their haunches watching them, then whistled loudly and plunged down the burrows into tunnels.

Lewis and Clark got some of their men to help them dig for specimens, but digging was futile. Finally, they filled a tunnel with water, forcing one of the creatures out. The French trappers who accompanied the Americans knew this animal well. *"Petit chien,"* they called it, meaning "little dog."

The animal was actually nothing like a dog; it was a member of the squirrel family. The men had a hard time settling on a name. Its bark reminded Lewis of a toy dog, but he

Prairie dogs sit on their haunches so they can keep an eye out for predators.

Three young prairie dogs gather at the entrance of a burrow.

preferred to call it the barking squirrel. Clark called it the burrowing squirrel and the ground rat. One man, Sergeant Ordway, insisted on calling it the prairie dog, the name that has stuck with it through two centuries.

A few days earlier, Clark had spotted a striking new creature. "Several wild goats seen in the plains. They are wild and fleet," he wrote. On September 14, Clark killed one of these "goats" and described it. He called it a goat but really couldn't figure out what it was, with its eyes like a sheep's and its body like an African antelope's. "Such an animal was never yet known in the U.S. states," wrote Sergeant Ordway. Perhaps it was a goat, but it lacked the beard typical of goats. The men struggled to find a name. They tried *cabre,* the Spanish word for goat, spelling it also *cabra, cabree,* and *cabrie.* Lewis, impressed by the animal's graceful fleetness, settled on "antelope." He wrote in his journal, "I beheld the rapidity of their flight along the ridge before me. It appeared rather [more like] the rapid flight of birds than the motion of quadrupeds," or four-legged animals.

Many people still use Lewis's name for it today, even though it is not scientifically correct. Scientists refer to it as the pronghorn, for this beautiful animal is unique in the world, not closely related either to goats or to antelope. No other animal has branching hollow horns that are shed every year. The pronghorn is the fastest running animal in America; it has been clocked at close to sixty miles an hour.

Pronghorn are especially fast runners.

The horns of the pronghorn are different from those of any other animal.

The mule deer lives in drier, rougher areas than the whitetail.

Three days after Clark had killed the first pronghorn, a hunter returned with a deer quite different from the familiar white-tailed deer. The new deer was about a third bigger than a whitetail. Its fur was a darker shade of gray and was thicker and longer than that of a whitetail. Its body was also stouter. The bucks were especially large. Lewis remarked on the animal's huge ears. One later specimen had ears almost a foot long. In his detailed description of this animal, Lewis called it the mule deer, an appropriate name that has stuck to this day.

The men learned more about the mule deer as they became familiar with it. Lewis wrote, "They prefer the open grounds and are seldom found in woodlands or river bottoms, and

[when] pursued, they invariably run to the hills or open country, as the elk do. The contrary happens with the common [white-tailed] deer." The men also noted that the mule deer "jumps like a goat or a sheep" instead of running like a white-tail. This kind of movement, springing off with all four feet at one time, is called stotting. Stotting enables the deer to bound easily over rocks and fallen logs.

On September 17, Lewis killed a magpie. Clark admired its greenish purple feathers and white markings. The magpie

The magpie that lives in North America is almost identical to that found in Europe.

was known in Europe, but it wasn't found east of the Mississippi River, so it was new to Lewis and Clark.

On the same day that he saw the magpie, Lewis wrote: "This scenery already rich, pleasing, and beautiful was still further heightened by immense herds of buffalo, deer, elk, and antelopes, which we saw in every direction feeding on the hills and plains. I do not think I exaggerate when I estimate the number of buffalo which could be comprehended at one view to amount to 3,000."

3

Buffalo, Ruler of the Prairie

The men had gotten their first taste of buffalo on August 23, after a member of their party shot one. It took twelve men to bring the carcass into camp. From then on, this magnificent animal often sustained the men as they crossed the prairies, just as it sustained the Native Americans who dwelled on the prairie and beyond. Some tribes living west of the Rocky Mountains traveled east to the prairie every year to hunt buffalo.

The abundance of buffalo, more correctly called the American bison, continually astonished the explorers. On their trip home in 1806, Clark wrote, "I ascended to the high country

Huge herds of bison once dominated the prairies.

and from an eminence I had a view of a greater number of buffalo than I had ever seen before at one time. I must have seen near 20,000 of these animals feeding on this plain."

Lewis and Clark were able to observe the natural behavior of buffalo before European Americans began to slaughter them. They noted that buffalo lived in small herds and that many herds could be seen feeding in the same area at one time, all moving in the same direction, as if part of a larger group. Lewis and Clark probably didn't notice the bison's annual pattern of migration across the prairie, since the expedition didn't stay long enough in a place where they could observe it.

The men enjoyed eating buffalo meat. But hunting buffalo wasn't always convenient for travelers on the river, and only thirty-five were killed during September and October 1804.

The Corps of Discovery spent the winter of 1804–1805 at a fort they built in what is now North Dakota. They named it Fort Mandan because it was near villages of the Mandan tribe. The Hidatsa Indians also lived nearby. During the winter, Lewis and Clark hired a French Canadian man named Toussaint Charbonneau as an interpreter. His pregnant teenage

The buffalo grazed in small herds that dotted the landscape.

Fort Mandan provided a home for the Corps of Discovery during the winter of 1804–1805. This reconstruction shows what it looked like.

wife, Sacagawea, belonged to the Shoshone tribe. She had been kidnapped several years earlier by the Hidatsa. The explorers would need to get horses from the Shoshone in order to cross the Rocky Mountains, and Sacagawea could help communicate with them.

During the long winter, the Americans learned much from the Mandan and Hidatsa about the importance of the buffalo to the Native Americans' survival. Lewis wrote in his journal about an Indian technique for killing buffalo. A swift-running, brave young man called a buffalo runner would disguise himself with a buffalo skin and wait between a herd of buffalo and a cliff. Other men got behind the herd and drove it forward, shouting and waving their robes. The buffalo runner dashed as fast as he could toward the cliff, leading the buffalo to their doom. When he reached the cliff, he scrambled over the edge and hid in a crevice. The buffalo galloped right over the precipice, falling to their death, and the hunters harvested the meat, hides, and other useful parts. Often, more buffalo died than the Indians could use, and the rest were left for the wolves and grizzly bears. The buffalo runner risked his life for the sake of the hunt. If he stumbled, he could be trampled, or he might lose his grip climbing into the crevice and, like the buffalo, fall to his death.

The Indians harvested as much as possible at these jumps. They butchered the bodies at the site and sliced the meat into

This painting by George Catlin (1832) shows Sioux Indians preparing buffalo hides and drying the meat. Their teepees are made of buffalo hides.

thin strips, hanging them in the sun to dry. The dried meat, called jerky, would last a long time. Some of the jerky was used to produce pemmican, an Indian food the explorers learned to make for themselves. To make pemmican, dried meat is pounded together with fat and bone marrow and, often, dried berries. When properly done, pemmican can last for years without refrigeration. The Indians also enjoyed fresh buffalo meat. The hump was a favorite of many tribes, as was the tongue.

Buffalo hides were used by tribes such as the Hidatsa, who lived along the river, to make small round boats called bull boats. A fresh hide was placed over a willow framework to dry. As it dried, the hide shrank, making a tight, waterproof covering. Bull boats were especially useful for quick trips across the river. The Corps of Discovery used them during their winter stay near the Hidatsa and Mandan and learned from the Indians how to make them. More than a year after leaving these tribes, Lewis's men made a bull boat and another, similar craft from buffalo hides and used them to travel down the Yellowstone River during the homeward stretch of their journey.

The whites learned from the Indians how to make their own moccasins and Indian-style clothing out of the hides of buffalo and other animals. Just like the Indians, the explorers

Buffalo robes provide great warmth.

used buffalo robes and hides as blankets, saddle blankets, and tents, and as tarpaulins to protect their gear from the rain. Even the horses might wear buffalo-hide moccasins when their feet got sore.

As winter melted into spring, Lewis and Clark prepared writings and scientific samples to send to Jefferson. They included mule deer antlers, specimens of insects and mice, stuffed male and female pronghorn and their skeletons, a coyote skeleton, and various animal skins. Lewis sent live animals, too—a prairie sharp-tailed grouse hen, a prairie dog, and four magpies. Only the prairie dog and one magpie made it to Jefferson alive.

On April 7, 1805, a crew of men left for St. Louis in the keelboat, taking the precious specimens, reports, and copies of journals with them. The rest of the expedition, now thirty-three people, headed onward. Traveling in six small canoes and the two pirogues, they continued up the Missouri River past the prairies and into the Rocky Mountains. The group included Charbonneau, Sacagawea, and their young son, named Jean Baptiste. After leaving Fort Mandan, Lewis, Clark, the Charbonneau family, and George Drouillard, another interpreter, slept in an Indian-style buffalo-hide teepee. The others had to sleep in the open, as their tents by this time had rotted and been torn to pieces.

Each spring, the Hidatsa and Mandan set fire to the prairie

*The Indians burned the prairie to encourage new grass to grow
and to keep trees from taking over.*

to encourage fresh, tender grass to grow. The young grass fed their horses and also attracted the buffalo. As the buffalo crossed the river on the unstable spring ice to reach the tempting new grass, one or two might get trapped on a piece of ice that broke free. The Indians, lying in wait for such an unfortunate animal, would rush out, using floating blocks of ice as stepping stones. As the buffalo stood helpless on its tipsy little island, an Indian would kill it, then paddle the block of ice to shore. The Indians also harvested carcasses of bison that had drowned and been frozen in the river ice during the winter.

Lewis thought of another way to utilize the bison. "I also saw several parcels of buffalo's hair hanging on the rose bushes, which had been bleached by exposure to the weather and become perfectly white. It had every appearance of the wool of the sheep, though much finer and more silky and soft. I am confident that an excellent cloth may be made of the wool of the buffalo," he wrote. Later on, a company did try to make buffalo cloth, but the project turned out to be unprofitable.

As the expedition continued across the prairie, it encountered more bison. Even though the Indians had been hunting them for many generations, the buffalo had little or no fear of people. On April 22, 1805, Lewis wrote, "Walking on the shore

Buffalo wool is very soft.

Buffalo mothers are very protective of their calves.

this evening I met with a buffalo calf which attached itself to me and continued to follow close at my heels until I embarked and left it."

On these vast prairies many bison must have lived their entire lives without encountering human hunters and learning to fear them. Lewis commented on May 4, 1805, "I saw immense quantities of buffalo in every direction. . . . Having an abundance of meat on hand I passed them without firing on them; they are extremely gentle—the bull buffaloes particularly will scarcely give way to you. I passed several in the open plain within fifty paces; they viewed me for a moment as something novel and then very unconcernedly continued to feed."

A few days later he wrote, "We saw a great quantity of game today, particularly elk and buffalo; the latter are now so gentle that the men frequently throw sticks and stones at them in order to drive them out of their way."

But buffalo could be dangerous, too. One night a bull crossing the river stumbled into one of the pirogues and panicked. He "ran up the bank in full speed directly towards the fires

The elk, also called wapiti, lives both on the prairies and in the forested mountains.

Bison bulls can weigh over a ton.

and was within eighteen inches of the heads of some of the men who lay sleeping before the sentinel could alarm him or make him change his course."

The buffalo also became an annoyance on the return trip. July was mating season, and Clark wrote, "The bulls keep up such a grunting noise which is [a] very loud and disagreeable sound that we are compelled to scare them away before we can sleep—the men fire several shot at them and scare them away."

4

Wolves and Coyotes, the Wild Dogs of the Plains

After leaving Fort Mandan, the explorers still had many miles of prairie to pass through before reaching the Rocky Mountains. They continued to observe and hunt the large-prey animals—buffalo, elk, deer, and pronghorn. But they and the Indians weren't the only hunters on the prairie.

The abundant game also served as food for wild hunters. The travelers saw wolves so consistently with bison that Lewis wrote, "The country in every direction around us was one

Wolves are highly social animals that live in family groups called packs.

vast plain in which innumerable herds of Buffalo were seen attended by their shepherds, the wolves." The wolves always seemed to hang around the game animals. Clark commented in his journal, "Wolves follow their [prey's] movements and feed upon those which die by accident or which are too poor to keep pace with the herd." The wolves didn't prey just on the halt and the lame, however. Lewis noted on April 29, 1805, how they hunted pronghorn: "They generally hunt in parties of six, eight, or ten; they kill a great number of antelopes at this season [early spring]; the antelopes are yet meager and the females are big with young; the wolves take them most generally in attempting to swim the river. . . . We have frequently seen the wolves in pursuit of the antelope in the plains; they appear to decoy a single one from a flock and then pursue it, alternately relieving each other until they take it."

Lewis described another way wolves had of hunting pronghorn, which was to take advantage of their curiosity: The pronghorn "sometimes leave their flock to go and look at the wolves, which crouch down, and, if the antelope be frightened at first, repeat the same maneuver, and sometimes relieve each other, till they decoy it from the party, when they seize it."

Wolves are hunters. They kill animals like deer and elk for food.

Wolves plagued the expedition by eating any carcass that wasn't brought in during the day it was hunted. Clark wrote, "All meat which is left out all night falls to the wolves which are in great numbers always in the neighborhood of the buffaloes." At a pile of drowned bison along a river, the men encountered a number of wolves that had been gorging on the carcasses. Clark stabbed a glutted wolf to death, using the sharp point of his staff.

Although wolves were common and unafraid of people, only once did a wolf attack the expedition. One night, a wolf bit an explorer on the hand as he slept. When the man woke up, the wolf tried to attack another and was shot to death. The wolf's behavior was very abnormal; perhaps it was ill.

The kind of wolf encountered by the Corps was later called the Great Plains or buffalo wolf. It differed from the familiar eastern timber wolf in several ways. As Lewis described it, "The large wolf found here is not as large as those of the Atlantic states. They are lower and thicker made, shorter legged. Their color, which is not affected by the seasons, is gray or blackish brown and every intermediate shade from that to cream colored white. . . . We scarcely see a gang of buffalo without observing a passel of those faithful shepherds on their skirts in readiness to take care of the maimed [and] wounded."

The once-abundant buffalo wolf lived throughout the prairies from Canada into Texas. Trapped, shot, and poisoned out

Lewis and Clark saw white wolves on the plains. White wolves are now rarely seen south of the Arctic.

Wolves come in many colors, including pure black.

of existence by the settlers who followed in Lewis and Clark's footsteps, it is now extinct.

The wolf shared the prairies with its smaller cousin, the coyote. The Corps of Discovery first met the coyote at the edge of the mixed-grass prairie. The men thought it was a kind of fox. But when Lewis finally shot one near the mouth of the Niobrara River, he realized it was more like a wolf than a fox and called it the prairie wolf. In the journals, the men sometimes referred to it as the small wolf to distinguish it from the much larger buffalo wolf. Even though they gave this animal the name *wolf,* Lewis and Clark noticed important differences in behavior between the two species. They never saw buffalo wolves digging dens, but they referred to the coyote as the "burrowing dog." Lewis wrote, "They usually associate in bands of ten or twelve, sometimes more, and burrow near some pass or place much frequented by game; not being able alone to take a deer or goat [pronghorn], they are rarely ever found alone but hunt in bands; they frequently watch and seize their prey near their burrows; in these burrows they raise their young and to them they also resort when pursued; when a person approaches them they frequently bark, their note being precisely that of a small dog."

Strangely, although they became well acquainted with the coyote as they traveled, Lewis and Clark never gave a detailed physical description of the animal. Their observations about

The coyote is a very adaptable animal that can live in grasslands and forests and even near cities.

how the coyotes on the plains hunted, however, are especially interesting. In most places where coyotes live today, they do not hunt in packs. The male and female raise the pups together, and once the young are full grown, they leave their parents. Before wolves were reintroduced into Yellowstone National Park in 1995, however, the coyotes there and in some other parts of Wyoming had taken to hunting in packs and bringing down relatively large animals, such as deer and bear cubs. These animals had revived the plains coyote's way of life.

5

Meeting the Grizzly

Today, the grizzly bear's haunts are in the high country and the forest. This powerful symbol of the wild is rarely seen at all, much less boldly and out in the open. Before European American settlement of the plains, however, grizzlies often ventured onto the prairies and acted unafraid of people. Signs of the presence of grizzlies appeared early in Lewis and Clark's journey. On September 1, 1804, Clark referred to a "White Bear Cliff," so named because a grizzly had been killed in a den there.

The names used then for the great bear are confusing.

This grizzly is a rich brown color.

Lewis and Clark referred to it most often as the white bear. It wasn't actually white, but it often had a much paler coat than the animal they knew from eastern North America—the black bear (another confusing name, since the black bear isn't always black!). They also called it the yellow bear, the brown bear, and the grizzly. But it's clear that when they used these names they were talking about the same species, named by scientists *Ursus horribilis.*

This grizzly with a light-colored body lives on the open ground in Alaska. The "white bears" seen by Lewis and Clark might have looked similar.

In October, hunters from the expedition wounded a "white bear" near present-day Bismarck, North Dakota. Clark commented that he saw fresh bear tracks "three times as large as a man's track." Since bears enter dens where they spend the winter, the Corps of Discovery encountered no more signs of bears until after they left Fort Mandan.

In April 1805, Lewis wrote, "We found a number of carcasses of the buffalo lying along the shore, which had been drowned by falling through the ice in winter. . . . We saw also many tracks of the white bear of enormous size, along the river shore and about the carcasses of the buffalo, on which I presume they feed. We have not as yet seen one of these animals, though their tracks are so abundant and recent. . . . The Indians give a very formidable account of the strength and ferocity of this animal, which they never dare to attack but in parties of six, eight, or ten persons, and are even then frequently defeated with the loss of one or more of their party."

On April 29, the explorers killed their first grizzly bear just west of the mouth of the Yellowstone River, close to the present-day border between North Dakota and Montana. Lewis was walking along the river with one of his men when they came across two bears. They shot and wounded both. One ran away; the other charged. "Fortunately [the bear] had been so badly wounded that he was unable to pursue so closely as to prevent my charging my gun; we again repeated our fire and killed him."

Guns in those days were very awkward to use. Modern bullets hadn't yet been invented. The Corps of Discovery had the most up-to-date guns available, but they were still quite primitive. Loading the gun meant first pouring a measured amount of gunpowder into the barrel, then placing a cotton patch

Ritch Doyle, who presents living-history portrayals of William Clark, aims a rifle like the ones used on the expedition.

over the muzzle of the gun and topping it with a lead ball. The ball was rammed in tightly, using the ramrod that was stored below the barrel. Next, a small amount of powder was placed on a small metal pan, where the hammer would strike it. Then the gun was cocked and fired. The hammer struck the powder in the pan, causing a spark that passed through a tiny hole in the side of the barrel to the gunpowder within. The powder exploded, propelling the lead ball through the barrel and out toward the target.

Even the best soldiers took at least thirty seconds to load and shoot, and a gun had to be reloaded before each shot. Imagine standing there, needing a steady hand to load the rifle, while an angry, wounded grizzly bear is charging you!

At first, the explorers thought the Indians exaggerated how fierce the grizzlies were and how hard it was to kill them. It didn't take long, however, for the travelers to find out for themselves. After killing the first bear, Lewis commented, "It is a much more furious and formidable animal [than the black bear] and will frequently pursue the hunter when wounded. It is astonishing to see the wounds they will bear before they can be put to death."

In his journal entry for May 14, 1805, Lewis described this encounter with a grizzly: "In the evening the men in two of the rear canoes discovered a large brown bear lying in the open grounds [this may have been a bear previously wounded by one of the men] . . . and six of them went out to attack him, all good hunters; they . . . got within 40 paces of him unperceived. . . . Four . . . fired nearly at the same time and each put his bullet through him, two of the balls passed through the bulk of both lobes of his lungs. In an instant the monster ran at them with open mouth, and the two who had reserved their

The claws and teeth of a grizzly are very impressive.

The powerful grizzly bear is often curious rather than afraid when it encounters interesting sights, sounds, and smells, as this Alaskan bear shows.

fires discharged their pieces at him as he came towards them. Both of them struck him, one only slightly and the other fortunately broke his shoulder. This however retarded his motion for a moment only."

The men ran, and the bear chased them. More and more bullets flew, but the grizzly kept attacking until it was finally shot through the head.

Lewis himself came dangerously close to being killed by a grizzly, partly because of his own carelessness. He had shot a bison and was watching it die. A grizzly came up quietly behind him, probably attracted by the smell of blood. By the time Lewis saw the bear, it was only about twenty steps away. Lewis raised his gun, then realized he'd forgotten to reload. He began to walk quickly toward the nearest tree. The bear charged, "open mouthed and full speed."

Lewis realized his chances would be better in the nearby river, where he could stand and the bear would have to swim. He plunged in waist deep and turned to face the grizzly, ready to stab it with the blade on the end of his staff. Fortunately, the bear turned and ran off. Lewis waded ashore and promptly reloaded his rifle, vowing that he would never again forget to reload immediately after firing.

After several encounters with grizzlies that were almost fatal to the men, Lewis wrote, "The white bear have become so troublesome to us that I do not think it prudent to send one man alone on an errand of any kind, particularly where he has to pass through the brush."

The expedition was now at the Great Falls of the Missouri River. The explorers had to travel on land, painstakingly portaging their canoes and supplies around the falls. It took them a month to travel just twenty-five miles. The banks of the river provided fine bear habitat. The grizzlies fed on buffalo

Giant Springs, behind this little waterfall, is part of the Great Falls area of the Missouri River around which the Corps of Discovery had to portage. Today, dams have tamed this once wild section of the river.

that had drowned by falling through the ice or while trying to swim the river. The brush along the river's edge also provided cover for them.

Grizzlies were so numerous in this area that the men had many chances to learn about them. Lewis noted that grizzlies are bigger than black bears and have bigger teeth and longer claws. He observed that they are more likely to feed on animals, that they spend less time in hibernation, and that, unlike black bears, they don't climb trees as adults. Today, grizzlies are normally seen singly, except for mothers with cubs. The Corps of Discovery, however, often saw groups of two or three bears together.

Lewis's description of the grizzly's range is especially interesting. After reaching the Pacific, he wrote, "The brown, white, or grizzly bear is found in the Rocky Mountains in the timbered parts of it on the westerly side but rarely. They are more common below the Rocky Mountains on the borders of the plains . . . near the water courses. They are by no means as plentiful on this side [the Pacific] as on the other."

From Lewis's writings it appears that the grizzly bear most abundantly inhabited the region where the prairie gave way to the Rocky Mountains. Once the explorers entered the mountains, they encountered few bears. Today, however, the grizzly in the lower forty-eight states is limited almost completely to wooded parts of the Rockies. The only area where it can safely leave the protection of the forest and wander onto the plains as it once did is in north-central Montana, along the eastern side of the Rockies. There, enough land is protected by the federal and state governments and by the Nature Conservancy for grizzlies to once more experience their traditional habitat.

A grizzly bear mother will defend her cubs fiercely.

The trouble that grizzlies gave the Corps of Discovery almost always was caused by the men attacking the bears, not the other way round. The only other time bears appeared to be a threat was when the men had killed some game and a bear got wind of it. Most grizzlies today keep to themselves in the forest and avoid contact with people. Only when they are surprised or associate people with food might they become dangerous, especially when a mother bear feels the need to protect her cubs.

6

Into the Mountains

Perhaps the most abundant wildlife the explorers encountered above the Great Falls were mosquitoes—clouds of hungry, buzzing, blood-sucking mosquitoes. Luckily, the men had a kind of mosquito netting to protect themselves at night, but during the day the insects attacked incessantly. "My dog even howls with the torture he experiences from them. . . . They are so numerous that we frequently get them in our throats as we breathe," wrote Lewis.

Not far above the Great Falls, the Missouri River bends toward the south as it flows down from more mountainous country. Bighorn sheep, abundant on the cliffs of the river, bounded effortlessly from rock to rock along the cliffs. The expedition passed through a spectacular gorge Lewis dubbed "the Gates of the Rocky Mountains," shortened today to Gates of the Mountains. "This evening we entered much the most remarkable cliffs that we have yet seen. These cliffs rise from the water's edge on either side perpendicularly to the height of 1200 feet. Every object here wears a dark and gloomy aspect. The towering and projecting rocks in many places seem ready to tumble on us," Lewis wrote.

Right after passing through the Gates of the Mountains, Lewis sighted a strange new bird. "I saw a black woodpecker

Rugged cliffs rise up from both sides of the Missouri River at the Gates of the Mountains.

(or crow) today, about the size of the lark woodpecker as black as a crow. I endeavored to get a shot at it but could not. It is a distinct species of woodpecker; it has a long tail and flies a good deal like the jay bird," he wrote.

Eventually, this pretty bird would become the only animal described along the journey that would be named for Lewis himself. Lewis saw the bird often in the mountains. But it was only on the return trip that he got his hands on specimens and could describe it in detail. He wrote very descriptively, saying of its pinkish breast: "a curious mixture of white and blood red which has much the appearance of having been artificially painted or stained of that color."

Lewis was an unusual man, and the bird named after him is an unusual woodpecker. It spends little time hammering away at trees and digging in wood for grubs, preferring instead to catch flies and crack acorns.

Lewis kept finding and describing new species. But as the plains ended and the mountains began, the now-familiar animals began to disappear. In late July, before the explorers reached Three Forks, where the Jefferson, Madison, and Gallatin Rivers, named by Lewis, join to form the Missouri, they saw the last of the buffalo herds until their return trip in 1806. Elk had become scarce as well. After Three Forks they saw no more grizzly bears until their return trip. They were entering new territory, the edge of the forested mountains.

Lewis's woodpecker looks quite different from other American woodpecker species.

Now the quest for new animals became less important to Lewis than the search for the Shoshone Indians. The Shoshone had lots of horses, and the Corps needed horses to get through the Rocky Mountains. On August 11, while Lewis and three of the men were looking for an old Indian road, they saw a lone Shoshone on horseback, but he turned and galloped away. The next day, the four men followed an Indian road toward the crest of the Continental Divide, "to the most distant fountain of the waters of the mighty Missouri, in search of which we have spent so many toilsome days and restless nights."

After drinking from the small, clear stream, they continued to the top and "discovered immense ranges of high mountains still to the West of us with their tops partially covered with snow." The men walked down the other side and drank from a creek whose waters flowed all the way to the far-off Pacific Ocean.

Finally, on August 13, the explorers and the Shoshone made contact. Lewis and his small group came across the Indians first. The Shoshone had not seen white men before, and they were excited by the unfamiliar presents Lewis gave them. That evening, one of the Indians gave Lewis a piece of roasted salmon. Lewis was thrilled. He wrote: "This was the first salmon I had seen and perfectly convinced me that we were on the waters of the Pacific Ocean."

The Indians were suspicious of Lewis and his men, fearing they were allies of the Blackfeet, an enemy tribe. But when Clark and the rest of the expedition caught up with the group, Sacagawea discovered that the Shoshone chief, Cameahwait, was her long-lost brother, whom she hadn't seen since being kidnapped. Finding his sister among the whites made Cameahwait happy to trade horses to them.

Lewis wrote a great deal about the lives of the Shoshone, including their uses for wild plants and animals. The tribe made clothing from the hides of pronghorn, beaver, bighorn sheep, deer, elk, fox, marmot, mountain goat, otter, weasel, and wolf. One special piece of clothing Lewis admired greatly was a kind of cloak called a tippet. Cameahwait made a gift to Lewis of a tippet fashioned from 140 ermine skins. The white ermine, with a black tip on the tail, is actually a weasel that is killed during the winter, when its coat is white. The ermine

Lewis wearing the tippet given to him by Cameahwait.

skins were formed into small rolls that cascaded down the back of the wearer, almost as far as the waist. The rolls were attached to an otter-skin collar adorned with shiny oyster or abalone shells from the Pacific.

The Shoshone relied on two main sources for animal food—salmon from rivers on the western side of the Continental Divide and bison from the plains on the eastern side. When the explorers came across the Shoshone, the Indians were just about to leave to hunt buffalo on the prairie. The people were very hungry and were surviving mostly on seeds, roots, and berries.

When the salmon were running, the Indians used hooks and complex fish traps to catch them, which Lewis described at length. He also listed the uses the Shoshone had for the buffalo, including halters made of buffalo hair for their horses.

Porcupine quills provided artistic material for several tribes, including the Shoshone. The quills were dyed black, blue, red, and yellow. The striking black-and-white fur of skunks adorned the moccasins of young braves, with the tail dragging along the ground behind the heel. Native Americans have always valued eagle feathers, and the Shoshone wove them into their own hair and into the manes and tails of their horses. Elk and grizzly bear teeth and fish vertebrae served as jewelry.

Animal parts were vital in war. Making a shield from buffalo hide was a complicated process that took days. The shield meas-

This beautiful pipe bag, made by the Yankton Sioux in 1940, uses flattened, dyed porcupine quills in the design.

ured about two and a half feet in diameter and was decorated with paint and feathers. Otter skins made fine quivers. Pronghorn hides, folded and refolded and glued together, formed armor for both warriors and horses.

The Shoshone had a few worn animal skins that Lewis could not identify. Experts today believe this was the mountain goat, which is actually a member of the antelope family. Lewis never saw it alive, but Clark once spotted one in the distance.

The Corps of Discovery spent more than two weeks in the vicinity of the Shoshone. During this time, Lewis saw another new bird that he thought was a kind of woodpecker. On the return trip he would collect specimens and describe in detail what we now call Clark's nutcracker, actually a member of the jay family.

The explorers left the Shoshone on September 13 with twenty-nine horses they had acquired from them. An Indian they called Old Toby served as their guide. Getting through the mountains proved difficult. But finally, on September 4, 1805, they reached the lovely small valley called Ross' Hole, where

Charles M. Russell imagined what the meeting of Lewis and Clark with the Salish at Ross' Hole might have been like in this 1912 painting.

The Corps of Discovery traveled close to Lolo Creek in Montana on their way to cross the Bitterroot Mountains.

they met a group of Salish Indians, from whom they acquired more horses, including three colts. The expedition still had to cross the rugged Bitterroot Mountains. Lewis had learned that finding game in the mountains could prove difficult. If they had to, they could kill the colts for food.

After traveling north through the Bitterroot Valley of what is now Montana, they turned into the mountains, planning to use an Indian trail. Every year the Nez Perce (pronounced "nez purse") tribe, which lived west of the mountains, crossed over it to hunt buffalo on the plains. The Nez Perce knew the trail well, but Old Toby wasn't as familiar with it, and at a critical point he missed it, leaving the ridge tops and heading down to the Lochsa River instead. After realizing the error, the Corps of Discovery had to struggle back up through the dense forest littered with fallen trees.

Lewis hadn't known that western mountains were so different from those in the East. Back there, mountains weren't so steep and rugged, and they consisted of just a single range. Western mountains went on and on, range after range. The dense forest held almost no game, and the men were hungry. By September 17, they had already been forced to kill the colts for food. An early snowstorm left them cold and wet, and they were exhausted from the effort of climbing up and down mountains littered with fallen timber. They didn't know when, or even if, they would find their way out of the mountains.

The men were horrified to see that the Bitterroots were not just a single chain of mountains. Instead, they consisted of range upon range that the men had to struggle through to reach the Pacific side of the Rockies.

It was decided that Clark would take six men and go on ahead, hoping to find food along the way, which they could leave for the others. As a small group, they would be able to travel more quickly.

The main group continued to struggle along the trail, with many men sick. On September 20, they came across most of a stray horse that Clark had killed and left for them. At least

A male Richardson's blue grouse raises his tail and puffs out his throat in a mating display.

they now had more to eat than the few grouse that usually made up a meal along with the distasteful portable soup Lewis had brought along for emergency rations.

Despite his exhaustion, Lewis took the time before sleeping that night to write in his notebook about seven different birds. One was the beautiful Stellar's jay, up to then unknown to science. Lewis also mentioned seeing three species of grouse: Richardson's blue grouse, Franklin's grouse, and the Oregon ruffed grouse. All of these were new to science.

Also on September 20, Clark and the advance party finally descended the mountains onto a grassland called Weippe (WEE-eyep) Prairie. There, they made contact with a band of Nez Perce. The Indians fed the hungry men some buffalo and dried salmon, as well as plant roots. The major root came from the lovely blue camas, which is a kind of lily.

Stellar's jay is a common bird in the Rockies. Lewis was the first to describe it. These jays are feeding on grain in the parking lot at Lolo Pass on the Montana-Idaho border, near where the Corps of Discovery struggled through the Bitterroot Mountains.

The Nez Perce Indians fed the starving men dried salmon and the roots of the blue camas. Camas in bloom makes a bright blue carpet across a meadow.

The next day, Lewis and the rest caught up with Clark and fed hungrily on the dried fish and roots. But the travelers' digestive systems weren't used to this very different diet. Many men, including Lewis, became ill. While the sick recovered, the Indians showed Clark and the other healthy men how to make canoes by burning out the centers of trees.

Game was scarce on the western side of the mountains. The diet of roots and fish continued, and Lewis was still sick. There was no time to waste, however, and on October 6, the men left their horses behind in care of the Nez Perce and loaded the canoes. The Corps of Discovery was once again under way. They sped down the Clearwater and Snake Rivers, through many difficult rapids, reaching the Columbia River on October 16.

7

Down the Columbia River

The Corps of Discovery spent a day and a half exploring before heading down the Columbia River toward the Pacific Ocean. Clark took a few men and went north up the river while Lewis took measurements to determine latitude and longitude. The men bought provisions from the Yakima and Wanapam Indians and shot some sage grouse. Once they got under way, they didn't want to have to spend any more time than necessary hunting and gathering on shore.

The eastern parts of present-day Oregon and Washington are quite arid. Little game and few food plants can live away

The Corps of Discovery descended the Clearwater River on their way to the Columbia.

Salmon, like these chum salmon in Alaska, swim up the rivers of their birth, leaping through rapids and waterfalls, to reach their spawning grounds. Salmon used to form the basis of the economy for Indians living along the Columbia River.

from the rivers. Most of the Indians lived along the waterways, which served not only as sources of water but of food and rapid transportation as well. Salmon was the key resource. Before the Columbia River was dammed during the twentieth century, countless salmon struggled up the river every year to spawn in the rivers and streams that feed the Columbia. Seven species of salmon and closely related trout helped fuel the Indian economy. The explorers described five species: king (also called Chinook), silver, and sock-eye salmon, and steelhead and

Yellowstone cutthroat trout. Along the Columbia, Lewis and Clark observed many Indian villages and camps where the people were busy drying salmon. Lewis referred to the king as the common salmon, for, as he wrote, it was the species that "extends itself into all the rivers and little creeks on this side of the Continent, and to which the natives are so much indebted for their subsistence." Not only is this species the king economically, it also is the largest, usually weighing about twenty pounds and sometimes reaching almost a hundred pounds.

The earliest king salmon run began in late March. These early fish might swim as much as a thousand miles to reach their spawning beds, which could be as far away as creeks in the Rockies. As the season wore on, different species joined the king, allowing the Indians to harvest this vital resource well into November.

The Indians caught the salmon in many different ways, then dried it and pounded it into a powder. They stored it in baskets lined with dried fish skins. Each basket could hold up to a hundred pounds of dried salmon, a very concentrated food. At just one location, Clark counted a hundred and seven baskets—about ten thousand pounds of dried fish.

Some of the salmon was stored for winter use. The Indians dug holes in the ground and lined them with fish skins. They then filled the holes with baskets of dried fish, covering the cache with more fish skins and a layer of soil about a foot

Paul Kane (1810–1871) painted this scene at Kettle Falls along the Columbia River. Salmon work their way up the river while Indians trap them from the shore.

thick. It is difficult to imagine the former abundance of this great resource, since today many of the salmon runs are extinct and others barely hang on.

Salmon also served as an important trade item. Every year, Rocky Mountain tribes would travel to a great Indian trade fair near Celilo Falls on the Columbia River. They brought camas root, horses, and other desirable commodities to trade for the salmon, as well as for other fish, shells, roots, and berries of the Columbia River Basin and the Pacific Coast.

Thousands of Indians took part in these trade fairs. After white men started coming by ship to trade along the coast, their trinkets also made it to the Indian market.

The Indian trade fair had finished for the year by the time the Corps of Discovery arrived, so the explorers missed seeing how much trading among tribes took place. But they could see how abundant the salmon were and how much work the Indians put into catching, drying, and storing this basic food.

Traveling by dugout canoe down the untamed Columbia proved to be a great adventure for the explorers. Luckily, they were able to make it through rapids that the Indians had been sure would overturn the canoes. Just below Celilo Falls, almost halfway from the mouth of the Snake River to the Pacific Ocean, Clark made a rare biological error in his journal. "Great numbers of sea otters in the river below the falls, I shot one in the narrow channel today which I could not get," he wrote. Even though Clark later realized he had made a mistake and noted it in a journal, some books still repeat the error. Sea otters do not leave the ocean for fresh water, but harbor seals sometimes do. These animals were actually harbor seals.

Soon the group passed through the Cascade Mountains, which divide eastern from western Washington and Oregon, leaving the arid, harsh climate of eastern Washington and entering a completely different world—moist, mild, and fertile.

West of the Cascade Mountains, the land is moist and lush.

On November 3, 1805, the explorers finally reached territory that had previously been visited by white men. On November 7, while camped on the Washington side of the river, Clark wrote in his journal, "Great joy in camp. We are in *View* of the *Ocean*, this great Pacific Ocean which we [have] been so long anxious to see." They were only in the mouth of the Columbia River, however, and it took another ten days to reach the actual coast.

The explorers camped on the Washington side of the river, at Cape Disappointment, before deciding to spend the winter on the Oregon side.

Once the explorers got close to the coast, they had to decide where to spend the winter. Storms kept them wet and miserable as they camped in various places on either side of the wide river estuary. During the search for a winter home, Clark made note of another animal new to science, the Columbian black-tailed deer. "The deer of this coast differ materially from our common [white-tailed] deer in as much as they are much darker, deeper bodied, shorter legged, horns equally branched from the beam, the top of the tail black from the root to the end. Eyes large, and [they] do not lope but jump."

These deer live in the thick forests and brushlands of the Pacific Coast, and the men hunted them that winter. Today, scientists call the black-tailed deer a subspecies of the mule deer.

8

The Long, Wet Winter

On December 8, 1805, the men began to build their winter home, Fort Clatsop, named for the local Indian tribe. It was about three miles up a small river from the Columbia. The thick forest provided building materials and a nearby spring gave clean, fresh water. The constant rain made building difficult, but finally the explorers were able to move in just before Christmas.

Lewis had written few entries in his journal for a long time, but he made up for it during the winter. Of the one hundred and six days the explorers spent along the coast, rain fell on

Fort Clatsop was home to the Corps of Discovery during the winter of 1805-1806. This reconstruction is near the original site.

ninety-six, and the sun peeked out on only six. Lewis spent hour after hour carefully writing up observations on the most important plants and animals he had found while crossing the continent. He wrote "biographies" of a hundred different kinds of animals, including birds, mammals, fish, reptiles, and invertebrates. Clark copied everything Lewis wrote in his own journal in case Lewis's journal got lost.

The explorers spent as much time indoors as possible during the miserable, wet winter.

Eleven of the mammals, eleven birds, and two of the fish described by Lewis that winter were previously unknown to science. Others were subspecies of familiar mammals like the elk, bobcat, striped skunk, badger, and various squirrels. Many of his portraits served as the basis for later scientific descriptions of the species.

Some of the new birds, too, were only subspecies. But others, such as the western grebe, ring-necked duck, and northwestern crow, were completely new to science. Lewis's observations also extended the known range of several birds, including the coot, blue-winged teal, and canvasback.

One impressive bird Lewis described is the whistling swan. Swans look pretty much alike to most people, with their pure white feathers and long, slender necks. Both native and European swans existed in the East, and most people didn't try to tell them apart, including Lewis. For most of the outbound trip, he just used the word *swan* when he saw these elegant

Coots, seen here walking on ice, were known before, but Lewis's observations extended their range.

The whistling swan, or tundra swan, lives in many parts of North America.

birds. But along the Columbia River, he realized that the swans he saw were of two sizes. He made the mistake of thinking the larger swan was the same as the kind he had seen in the East, so he identified only the smaller one as a new species. He struggled to put the sounds it made into words: "Its note . . . cannot be justly imitated by the sound of letters, nor do I know any sounds with which a comparison would be pertinent. It begins with a kind of whistling sound and terminates in a round full note which is rather louder than the whistling. From the peculiar whistling of the note of this bird I have called it the whistling swan." Nowadays, this lovely bird is officially called the tundra swan instead of the whistling swan.

While Lewis wrote in his journal, many of the men hunted. Lewis worried almost every day that there would not be enough food to go round. Many a meal consisted of partly spoiled meat or fish. At first elk were common near the fort, but as the winter wore on, they moved farther and farther away, making it difficult to feed the explorers well. Carrying meat and hides back to the fort on their backs was difficult work for the men. And they had to hurry, as the meat spoiled quickly in the wet, mild weather. Still, elk formed the foundation of their diet, supplemented by some deer and a few

Trumpeter swans live only in the West.

The Roosevelt elk lives along the northern Pacific Coast.

beaver and otter, as well as fish and dogs purchased from the Clatsop Indians.

From December 1805 through March 20, 1806, the hunters managed to kill 131 elk. These were what are now called Roosevelt elk, a subspecies of the elk the men knew so well from the prairies. Besides meat, this animal provided the explorers with hides for making clothing and moccasins. Exposure to water while navigating rivers and the constant rain on the coast had ruined their clothing. A problem arose, however, in curing the hides. Brains from the animals are used in curing, but not enough brains were available to cure all the hides. Ultimately, however, the men made more than 330 pairs of moccasins as well as shirts and leggings. Lewis also used elk skins to make harnesses for the pack horses they would be using when they crossed back over the mountains in the spring. Elk

The men spent much of the winter making moccasins for the return journey.

fat served as material for making candles in molds that Lewis had brought along.

In January 1806, a dead whale washed ashore along the coast. By the time the explorers got to it, the Clatsop had already stripped the meat and blubber from the carcass, so the whites bought some of the meat and oil from them. The change in diet was very welcome and brought a small joke for the leaders, who wrote in their journals, "Small as the store is, we prize it highly, and thank the hand of providence for directing the whale to us, and think him much more kind to us than he was to Jonah, having sent this monster to be *swallowed by us* instead of *swallowing of us* as Jonah's did."

Later in the winter, the Fort Clatsop diet included some delicious variations. One day in February, a group of Indians came to visit, bringing along otter-skin hats and fish to sell. One of these was the eulachon (YOU-leh-kon). These foot-long fish start running up the rivers to spawn in February. When they begin their journey, their bodies are so full of fat that "when dried and a wick drawn through the body, they may be used as candles," resulting in their other name, candlefish.

Lewis wrote a detailed description and included a sketch in his journal. "I find them best when cooked in Indian style, which is by roasting a number of them together on a wooden spit without any previous preparation. . . . I think them superior to any fish I ever tasted, even more delicate and luscious

Lewis drew a picture of the eulachon in his notebook.

than the white fish of the lakes which have heretofore formed my standard of excellence among the fishes."

The other fish brought that day by the Indians was the white sturgeon, which is the largest of all freshwater fish. It can reach eleven feet in length and weigh almost a ton.

9

The Journey Home

The Corps of Discovery left Fort Clatsop on March 23, 1806. Despite many illnesses suffered and cold and wet weather endured, everyone had made it through the winter. The store of supplies, however, was greatly reduced. Virtually all the trade goods were gone, and just about all of their original clothing had worn out or rotted away. The men still had ammunition for their rifles, most of the scientific instruments, cooking kettles, and some dried roots and fish, but little more. They would have to feed themselves from the land as they traveled east.

Fortunately for Lewis, most of his scientific instruments, like a sextant and compass, survived to help him find the way for the entire trip.

Now the explorers had to struggle against the current of the great Columbia River and portage their canoes past the many rapids. In early May, the group arrived back at the Clearwater River, where the Nez Perce Indians had kept their horses for the winter.

The winter had been especially severe, and snow still lay deep upon the mountains. Lewis described it as "that icy

Clark's nutcracker is another western bird described by Lewis.

barrier which separates us from my friends and country, from all which makes life estimable." Nothing could be done to hurry the arrival of spring, but Lewis made good use of the time by writing more observations on animals in his journal.

Because they are named after the leaders, Lewis's woodpecker and Clark's nutcracker are of special interest to historians. During the layover with the Nez Perce, Lewis obtained several specimens of both birds and described them in detail. He also wrote of the beautiful western tanager, another bird new to science.

When the Corps of Discovery arrived in the Bitterroot Mountains,
they found deep snow.

Lewis spent time pondering the many colors of the grizzly bear. The men brought in a number of carcasses, so he could study the coats in detail. Was he seeing separate species of bears that have different colors? After examining animals ranging from almost white to jet black and finding no two pelts with exactly the same color, Lewis wrote, "Perhaps it would not be inappropriate to designate them the variegated bear," and he concluded, "If we were to attempt to distinguish them by the colors and to denominate each color a distinct species, we should soon find at least twenty."

Impatience to reach home overcame common sense, and the Corps of Discovery took off on their horses on June 10. They waited at Weippe Prairie for the young Nez Perce Indians who were supposed to guide them through the forbidding Bitterroot Mountains, but the guides didn't show up. On June 15, the explorers set out into the mountains during a drenching rainstorm. It turned out that they should have heeded the Indians' warning—the snow was still deep, and the explorers risked death by trying to proceed without guides. They cached, or hid, much of their food and baggage and retreated to Weippe Prairie.

Three Nez Perce agreed to lead them through the mountains in exchange for rifles. With the Indians' help, the Corps made it through the mountains in only seven days. After two days of reorganizing at Travelers' Rest, a campsite they had

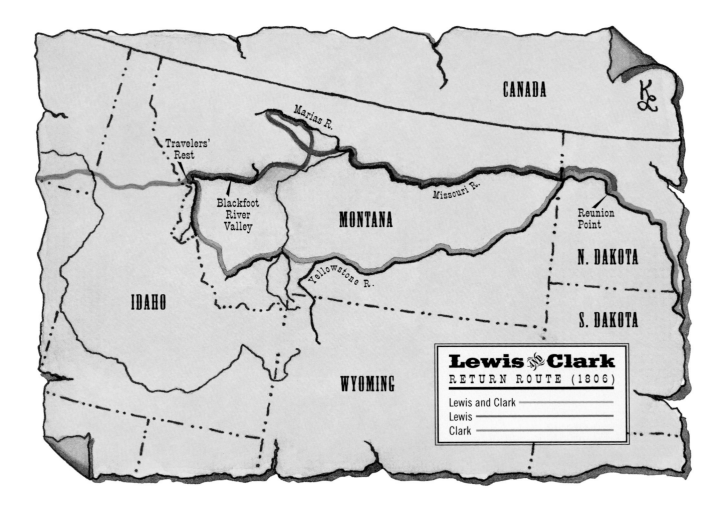

used on the westward trip, the explorers split up on July 3. Lewis and nine other men took a direct route, using Nez Perce guides. Clark and the rest of the party went by way of Three Forks and the Yellowstone River.

As Lewis traveled eastward up the Blackfoot River Valley, he observed a large colony of breeding pigeons. No one knew up to then that the passenger pigeon nested west of the Continental Divide. He also noted large numbers of wild horses.

Meanwhile, Clark's group was making its way to the Yellowstone River, encountering abundant game. "For me to mention or give an estimate of the different species of wild animals on this river, particularly buffalo, elk, antelopes, and wolves, would be incredible. I shall therefore be silent on the subject further," he wrote.

Buffalo were also on the move, swimming across the river in great herds and threatening to trample the Corps' camps dur-

Buffalo are comfortable in the water.

Bighorn sheep still live in many places in the Rocky Mountains.

ing the night. At one point the men encountered a huge herd crossing the river and had to wait an hour for it to pass by.

Clark commented on the abundance of other creatures, too. He saw a herd of forty bighorn sheep and managed to get samples of skin, bone, and heads. Birds such as crows, geese, hawks, larks, and passenger pigeons appeared in great numbers.

On August 12, Lewis's group reunited with Clark's. Lewis and his men had had their own adventures, including a run-in with a group of Blackfeet Indians, which resulted in the death

Huge flocks of waterfowl like these snow geese were common in Lewis's day.

of one of the Indians. Lewis had also been injured in a hunting accident, shot in the rear, and unable to move for many days.

After a brief stop at Fort Mandan, where they bid farewell to Charbonneau, Sacagawea, and young Jean Baptiste, the group continued down the Missouri, arriving back at St. Louis on September 21, 1806.

The Fate of the Journals and Specimens

When the Corps of Discovery finally showed up, people were amazed and delighted. The explorers had been gone for so long that it was feared they had all died. Since May 1805, when the keelboat carrying specimens and reports had come down the river from Fort Mandan, people had received only vague comments passed on from tribe to tribe about a group of white men traveling west.

Lewis, Clark, and Jefferson all wanted the journals from the great voyage of exploration to be published as soon as possible. But for many reasons, this did not happen. Several incomplete versions were published over the years, but most of the natural history information was left out. Only recently, between 1987 and 1999, was a complete set of the journals published. Thanks to the efforts of historian Gary Moulton, people could finally know the extent of the scientific observations and records made by the Corps of Discovery, especially by Meriwether Lewis himself.

The specimens from the journey, which represented many of the new kinds of vertebrate animals the explorers had described, met with indifferent fates, despite their importance. In addition to the animals, Lewis and Clark identified 178 new plants. They also wrote observations of many Indian tribes that they encountered.

Some of the live zoological specimens, including the prairie dog and magpie that miraculously survived a journey of more than four thousand miles under very rugged conditions, ended up in the Peale Museum in Philadelphia. The museum, run by artist Charles Willson Peale and his son, Rembrandt, was housed in Independence Hall. Thousands of specimens made up the collection, ranging from insects to stuffed mammals and skins of birds, as well as numerous minerals and preserved fish and snakes. Both the prairie dog and the magpie seem to have survived into the spring of 1806. After that, mention of the rodent ceases. Charles Peale mounted the magpie after it died.

When Lewis returned with the specimens from the greater part of the journey, he took them to Philadelphia. Alexander Wilson, a self-educated artist and naturalist, was in the process of putting together an illustrated book of birds of the United States. Wilson took an interest in the birds Lewis had obtained. He not only drew three of Lewis's birds, he also wrote scientific descriptions and gave the birds scientific names. These

Lewis requested that Alexander Wilson, a famous wildlife artist, make drawings of the bird specimens Lewis had brought back. Wilson ended up doing just three: the western tanager (upper left), Lewis's woodpecker (right), and Clark's nutcracker (below).

were the western tanager, Lewis's woodpecker, and Clark's nutcracker, which he called Clark's crow.

Until this time, American scientists hadn't devoted much attention to writing scientific descriptions and giving Latin names to plants and animals. But after seeing the new species that the Corps of Discovery had found in the West, several scientists got interested, and they went on to place them firmly in the scientific literature, basing their descriptions largely on Lewis's writings and on the specimens he collected. By 1823, scientists had described and given scientific names to twenty-one of the expedition's species. Others were named later.

Unfortunately, the only actual specimen Lewis collected that still can be identified is a scruffy-looking specimen of Lewis's woodpecker, which resides in the Museum of Natural History at Harvard University. Not everyone is convinced that it was collected by Lewis. But the lack of actual specimens is not as important as the lasting value of the descriptions of their appearance and behavior that Lewis and sometimes Clark painstakingly wrote in their journals. Their discoveries inspired other adventurous naturalists, including John James Audubon, to head west and study the abundant nature of the region.

Thanks to Lewis and Clark's journey, we have a record of what parts of North America were like before European American settlement.

To Learn More

I relied on many sources for information in writing this book, including Stephen Ambrose's fine biography of Meriwether Lewis, *Undaunted Courage* (New York: Simon & Schuster, 1996). Raymond Darwin Burroughs quotes extensively from the journals about the many animals described by Lewis and Clark in *The Natural History of the Lewis and Clark Expedition* (East Lansing, Michigan: Michigan State University Press, 1961), while Paul Russell Cutright chronicles the plants and animals in *Lewis & Clark: Pioneering Naturalists* (Lincoln, Nebraska: University of Nebraska Press, 1989). *Lewis and Clark Among the Indians*, by James P. Ronda (Lincoln, Nebraska: University of Nebraska Press, 1984), tells of the interactions of the explorers with the Indians. Daniel B. Botkin uses the Lewis and Clark expedition as a way of looking at conservation issues today in *Our Natural History: The Lessons of Lewis and Clark* (New York: The Berkley Publishing Group, 1995).

The complete journals have been faithfully transcribed from the originals and edited by Gary E. Moulton, who also provides extensive notes (*The Journals of the Lewis & Clark*

Expedition, Volumes 1-12, Lincoln, Nebraska: University of Nebraska Press, 1987-1999). For a selection of entries from the journals, see *The Journals of Lewis and Clark,* Bernard De Voto, editor (New York: Mariner Books, 1997).

Many guide books are available for families who want to explore the Lewis and Clark Trail, which has been designated a National Historic Trail. Museums and other sites along the way have exhibits filled with artifacts and fascinating information. *Along the Trail with Lewis and Clark,* second edition by Barbara Fifer and Vicky Soderberg (Helena, Montana: Montana Magazine/Farcountry Press, 2001), has lots of quotations from the journals and excellent maps prepared by Joseph Mussulman, as well as abundant information about sites along the way.

I am the author and William Muñoz the photographer of two other books about Lewis and Clark, tentatively titled *The Lewis and Clark Trail, Then and Now* (New York: Dutton Children's Books, to be published 2002), which tells of the differences in life and landscape between 1804-1806 and today, and *Plants on the Trail with Lewis and Clark* (New York: Clarion Books, 2003), which describes the plants they found and used, including plants that played an important role in the lives of the Indians. *The Incredible Journey of Lewis and Clark,* by Rhoda Blumberg (Magnolia, Massachusetts: Peter Smith Publishers, 1999), is an award-winning book for young people that gives an overall view of the expedition.

For those who explore the internet, "Lewis & Clark on the Information Superhighway" *(http://www.lcarchive.org/full-list.html)* provides links to every site on the web that concerns Lewis and Clark. A couple of especially good sites are "Discovering Lewis and Clark" *(http://www.lewis-clark.org)* and the official home of the Lewis and Clark Trail Heritage Foundation, Inc. *(http://www.lewisandclark.org)*. I have information about my own experiences along the trail on my web site, *http://www.dorothyhinshawpatent.com.*

Chronology of Animal Discoveries New to Science

The following list tells where the 121 new species and sub-species of vertebrate animals identified by Lewis and Clark were first seen or mentioned in their journals. Many books also include the hairy woodpecker (Cutright calls it "Cabanis's woodpecker"), making a total of 122 animals. However, the journal reference—"a small black and white woodpecker with a red head"—is quite vague and could apply to either the hairy or the downy woodpecker, so I have omitted it. I want to thank Chuck Sundstrom for his hard work in compiling the list, which I have modified.

1804
WOOD RIVER

May 3	Missouri beaver	Platte County, Missouri
May 18	Plains horned toad	Missouri River; specimen shipped to Jefferson before the expedition started up the Missouri River.

Up the Missouri River

May 30	Great Plains wolf	Missouri River, Kansas
May 31	Eastern wood rat	Mouth of Osage River, Missouri
June 13	Raccoon (new subspecies)	Chariton River, Missouri
July 3	Channel catfish	Above Platte River
August 5	Bull snake	Near Niobrara River, South Dakota and Nebraska
	Least tern	Missouri River, Nebraska and Iowa
August 25	Blue catfish	Missouri River, near Vermillion River, South Dakota
September 7	Black-tailed prairie dog	Missouri River, Boyd County, South Dakota
September 12	Prairie sharp-tailed grouse	Missouri River, South Dakota
September 14	Pronghorn	Mouth of Ball Creek, South Dakota
	White-tailed jackrabbit	Missouri River, Chamberlain, South Dakota
September 15	Desert cottontail rabbit	White River, South Dakota
September 16	Black-billed magpie	Missouri River, South Dakota
September 17	Mule deer	Missouri River, South Dakota
September 18	Coyote	Missouri River, South Dakota
October 18	Poor-will	Cannonball River, South Dakota
November 9	Long-tailed weasel	Fort Mandan, North Dakota

1805

April 7	Northern bobcat	Fort Mandan, North Dakota
	Short-tailed shrew	Fort Mandan, North Dakota

April 9	Pocket gopher	Knife River, North Dakota
April 10	Praire horned lark	Fort Mandan, North Dakota
April 11	Northern flicker	Missouri River, reported at Fort Mandan
April 14	Montana horned owl	Above Little Missouri River, North Dakota
April 17	Long-billed curlew	Missouri River, in Western North Dakota
April 26	Audubon's mountain sheep	Mouth of Yellowstone River, North Dakota

INTO MONTANA

April 29	Grizzly bear	Big Muddy Creek, Montana
May 3	Yellow-haired porcupine	Poplar River, Montana
May 5	Hutchin's goose	Mouth of Poplar River, Montana
May 9	Western willet	Missouri River, above Poplar River, Montana
May 10	Shira's moose	Mouth of Milk River, Montana
May 25	Striped skunk (subspecies)	Musselshell River, Montana
May 26	Soft-shelled turtle	Bull Wacker Creek, Montana
June 4	McCown's longspur	Marias River, Montana
June 5	Sage grouse	Marias River, Montana
June 8	Pale American goldfinch	Marias River, Montana
June 10	White-rumped shrike	Marias River, Montana
June 11	Goldeye	Missouri River, above Marias River, Montana
	Sauger	Missouri River, above Marias River, Montana

June 13	Cutthroat trout	Great Falls, Montana
June 15	Prairie rattlesnake	Great Falls, Montana
June 22	Western meadowlark	Great Falls, Montana
June 25	Brewer's blackbird	Great Falls, Montana
	Water terrapin	Great Falls, Montana
June 30	Pacific nighthawk	Great Falls, Montana
July 6	Swift fox	Great Falls, Montana
July 8	Thirteen-lined ground squirrel	Great Falls, Montana
July 20	Lewis's woodpecker	Gates of the Mountains, Montana
	Pack rat	Gates of the Mountains, Montana
July 21	Richardson's blue grouse	Missouri River, north of Helena, Montana
July 23	Western hognose snake	Missouri River, near Townsend, Montana
July 24	Western garter snake	Missouri River, near Townsend, Montana
August 1	Piñon jay	Jefferson River, Montana

ACROSS THE CONTINENTAL DIVIDE AND ON THE LOLO TRAIL

August 20	Yellow-bellied marmot	Shoshone Indian territory, Idaho
	Ermine	Lemhi River, Idaho
August 22	Clark's nutcracker	Lemhi River, Idaho
August 24	Mountain goat	Lemhi River, Idaho
September 20	Oregon ruffed grouse	Lolo Trail, Idaho
	Franklin's grouse	Lolo Trail, Idaho
	Stellar's jay	Lolo Trail, Idaho

WASHINGTON AND OREGON

October 20	Double-crested cormorant	Below Umatilla River, Oregon
October 23	Harbor seal	Narrows of Columbia River, 100 miles inland
Fall	Columbian white-tailed deer	Washington and Oregon
November 11	White sturgeon	Cape Disappointment, Washington
November 19	Columbian black-tailed deer	Cape Disappointment, Washington
November 20	Sea otter	Baker's Point, Washington
November 29	Western crow	Tongue Point, Astoria, Oregon
December 2	Roosevelt elk	Tongue Point, Astoria, Oregon

1806

January 3	Oregon jay	Not found at but described at Fort Clatsop, Oregon
February 21	Great-tailed (red) fox	Not found at but described at Fort Clatsop, Oregon
	Oregon bobcat	Fort Clatsop, Oregon
February 24	Candlefish (Eulachon)	Fort Clatsop, Oregon
February 25	Townsend's chipmunk	Fort Clatsop, Oregon
	Western gray squirrel	Not found at but described at Fort Clatsop, Oregon
	Douglas's squirrel	Not found at but described at Fort Clatsop, Oregon
	Richardson's squirrel	Not found at but described at Fort Clatsop, Oregon

February 26	Mountain beaver	Fort Clatsop, Oregon
	Western badger	Not found at but described at Fort Clatsop, Oregon
	Townsend's mole	Not found at but referred to at Fort Clatsop, Oregon
February 28	Striped skunk (subspecies)	Not found at but referred to at Fort Clatsop, Oregon
March 1	Columbian sharp-tailed grouse	Not found at but described at Fort Clatsop, Oregon
March 3	Dusky horned owl	Clearwater River, Idaho; described at Fort Clatsop, Oregon
	Western American raven	Not found at but described at Fort Clatsop, Oregon
	Northwestern crow	Not found at but described at Fort Clatsop, Oregon
March 4	Western pileated woodpecker	Not found at but described at Fort Clatsop, Oregon
	Western winter wren	Not found at but described at Fort Clatsop, Oregon
March 7	Pacific fulmar	Fort Clatsop, Oregon
	Pacific loon	Fort Clatsop, Oregon
	Glaucous-winged gull	Fort Clatsop, Oregon
	Western gull	Fort Clatsop, Oregon
	Bonaparte's gull	Fort Clatsop, Oregon
	Western grebe	Not found at but described at Fort Clatsop, Oregon
March 8	Lesser Canada goose	Not found at but described at Fort Clatsop, Oregon

March 9	Whistling swan	Not found at but described at Fort Clatsop, Oregon
March 10	Red-necked grebe	Not found at but described at Fort Clatsop, Oregon
March 11	California newt	Columbia River (Grand Rapids), Washington
March 13	Starry flounder	Fort Clatsop, Oregon
	Steelhead trout	Fort Clatsop, Oregon
March 15	White-fronted goose	Not found at but described at Fort Clatsop, Oregon

HOMEWARD BOUND

March 28	Ring-necked duck	Not found at but described at Fort Clatsop, Oregon
	Northwestern garter snake	Columbia River (Deer Island), Washington
March 29	Western frog	Columbia River, near Lewis's River, Washington and Oregon
April 5	Harris's woodpecker	Not found at but referred to near Willamette River, Oregon
April 7	Mountain quail	Washougal River, Oregon and Washington
April 16	Oregon pronghorn	Below Celilo Falls, Oregon
April 24	Western fence lizard	Near Roosevelt, Washington
	Yellow-bellied marmot (subspecies)	John Day River, Washington
April 25	North Pacific rattlesnake	Near Roosevelt, Washington
April 26	Columbia River chub	Mouth of Umatilla River, Washington and Oregon
April 29	Northern squawfish	Walla Walla River, Washington

IDAHO

May 27	Columbian ground squirrel	Camp Chopunnish, Idaho
May 29	Pigmy horned toad	Camp Chopunnish, Idaho
May 30	Columbian toad	Clearwater River, Idaho
	Pacific tree frog	Camp Chopunnish, Idaho
June 6	Western tanager	Camp Chopunnish, Idaho
June 15	Hairy woodpecker	Lolo Trail, Idaho
	Broad-tailed hummingbird	Hungry Creek on Lolo Trail, Idaho

MONTANA

July 1	Western mourning dove	Lolo Creek (Travelers' Rest), Montana
July 16	Mountain sucker	Yellowstone River, Montana
August 7	Forster's tern	Mouth of Yellowstone River, North Dakota

INDEX

Page numbers in **bold** type refer to illustrations.